BLUE SKY
WHITE STARS

SARVINDER NABERHAUS

Illustrated by

KADIR NELSON

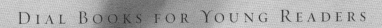

DIAL BOOKS FOR YOUNG READERS

BLUE SKY

WHITE STARS

BLUE SKY

WHITE

STARS

RED ROWS

RED ROWS

WHITE ROWS

WHITE ROWS

RED, WHITE, AND BLUE

OLD
GLORY

OLD
GLORY

Sea waves

See waves

SEW TOGETHER
WON NATION

So together
One nation

WELL
WORN

WELL
WORN

WOVEN
TOGETHER

ALL AMERICAN

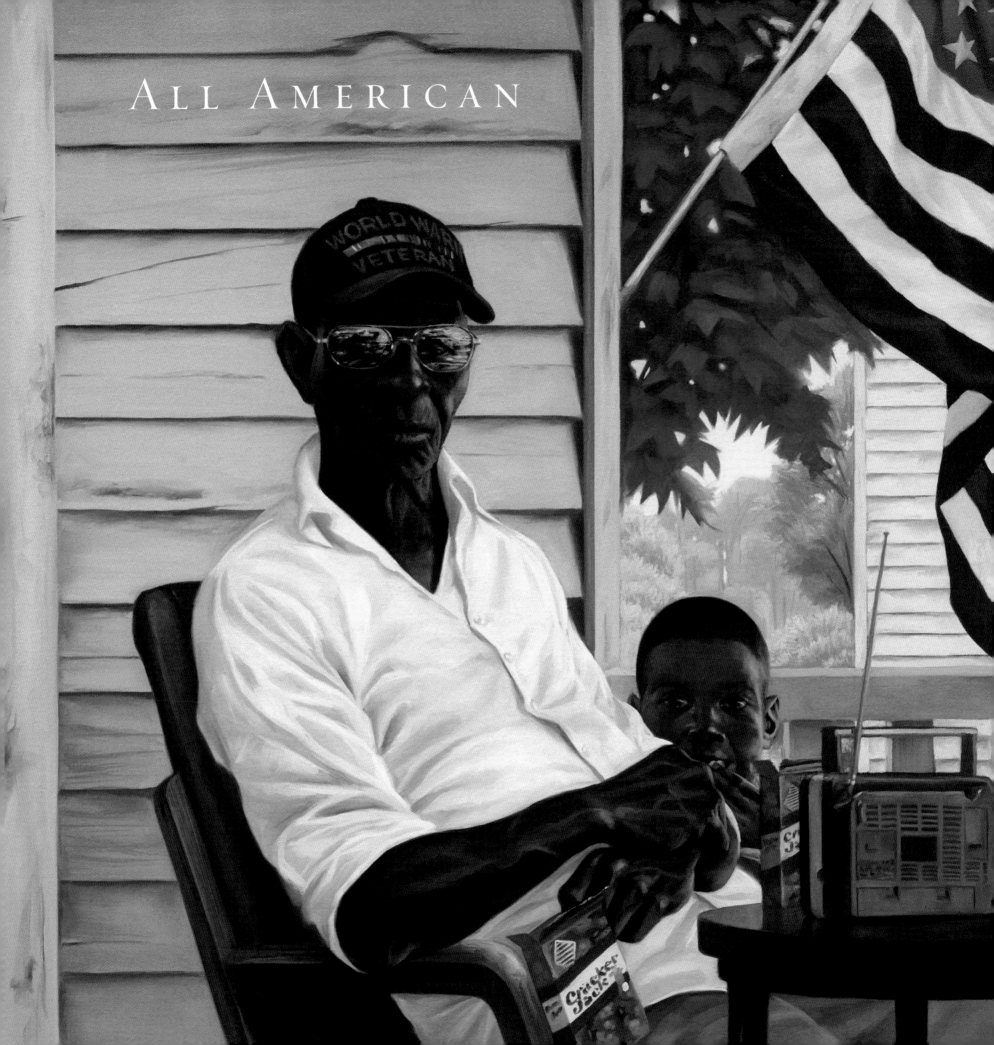

ALL AMERICAN

S TAND
PROUD

R I S I N G   U P

R ISING   UP

Fly high

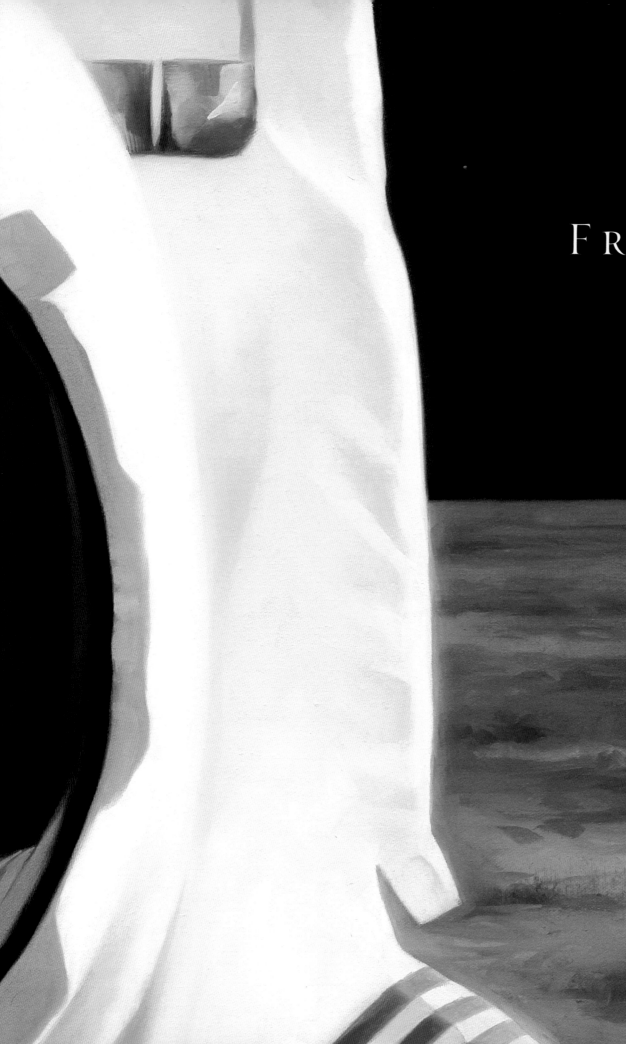

FREEDOM

RED, WHITE, BLUE

SKY, WHITE STARS

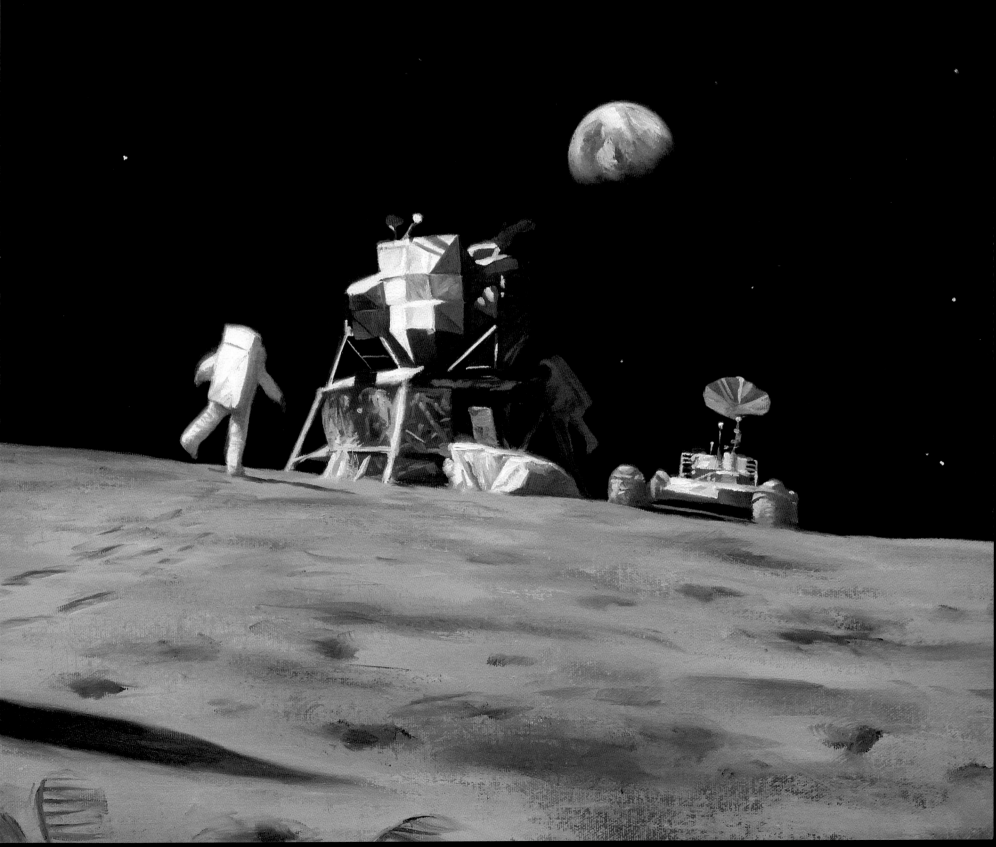

FOREVER

To Goga, Jyoti, Nick, Tom, and Ruth,
and all the generations of immigrants
—S.N.

For every American, Life, Liberty,
and the Pursuit of Happiness
—K.N.

A NOTE FROM THE AUTHOR

This story was written as a parallel between America and its flag—the same words describe both. I began this book thinking of the deep blue sky dotted with white stars that early immigrants to this country saw as they boarded ships headed toward religious freedom in the New World.

In the early 1920s my great-grandfather, Boota Singh Bal, boarded a ship to come to America but at the last minute changed his mind. My dad wished he had stayed on the boat and embarked on the journey. It was my dad's dream to come to America, which he achieved through a veterinary medicine scholarship. In 1965, when I was nearly four years old, my family left Punjab, India, and traveled over 7,000 miles to join my father. Thus began my lifelong journey assimilating into the culture that fostered the American dream, eventually becoming a citizen in 1996. Like my dad, I've followed my dreams which led me to this story, where blue sky is filled with white stars.

ACKNOWLEDGMENTS

I want to acknowledge Ann Green for her immeasurable help with *Blue Sky*. I also want to acknowledge the Bal family, Harpal and Harbhajan, who brought me to this country; my kids and husband, as well as the Randhawa family and Naberhaus family. A special thanks to Lucia Monfried, Lauri Hornik, Jenny Kelly, Kadir Nelson, Ammi-Joan Paquette, my online critique groups, Write Away (Jody, Sandy, Suzanne, Jill, Kerry, Diana) and the Ames group (including Susan Schmid).

A NOTE FROM THE ILLUSTRATOR

I am very proud to have created this series of paintings illustrating Sarvinder Naberhaus's poetic celebration of the American flag. I was immediately struck by the author's sparse yet rousing text—its simplicity and power; its beautifully drawn parallels between the American landscape and the diversity of its people, and the symbolism stitched into the fabric. It is the American ideals that have continued to echo in our hearts and minds throughout our tumultuous history.

With each painting, I was inspired to remind readers of the resilience of American principles, and that as we continue to push forward, our strength lies in our willingness to embrace our differences. I hope this work will always remind us that our ever-evolving country was forged by—and for—people from all walks of life and every background, and that our future as a nation hinges on Abraham Lincoln's enduring admonition that, "a house divided cannot stand." The American flag is a shining symbol that calls us to remember that we have the potential to uphold the promise of "Life, Liberty, and the Pursuit of Happiness," together. Only together . . .

NOTES PROVIDING BACKGROUND MATERIAL ABOUT THE FLAG AND OTHER PATRIOTIC SYMBOLS AND THE MEANING OF THE PHRASES IN THIS BOOK ARE AVAILABLE ON THE AUTHOR'S WEBSITE.

Dial Books for Young Readers | Penguin Young Readers Group | An imprint of Penguin Random House LLC | 375 Hudson Street, New York, NY 10014
Text copyright © 2017 by Sarvinder Naberhaus. Illustrations copyright © 2017 by Kadir Nelson. Penguin supports copyright. Copyright fuels creativity, encourages diverse voices, promotes free speech, and creates a vibrant culture. Thank you for buying an authorized edition of this book and for complying with copyright laws by not reproducing, scanning, or distributing any part of it in any form without permission. You are supporting writers and allowing Penguin to continue to publish books for every reader. CIP Data is available. Printed in China | ISBN 9780803737006 | Design by Jennifer Kelly | Text set in Requiem Fine
The interior artwork was created in oils on canvas. The front and back covers were created in oils on panel.